MONEY 101: earn, give, save, spend.

BOOK ONE IN THE SERIES:

REAL, BASIC, RELEVANT LIFE SKILLS *for Our Children*

BY MIKE CHENEY

PUBLISHED BY

Money 101: Earn, Give, Save, Spend.

Book One in the Series:
Real, Basic, Relevant Life Skills for Our Children

ISBN: 978-1-7335501-0-9

Project Managing Designer, Cover, and Interior Layout: Ian Serff (serffcreative.com)
Production: Zane McMinn, Comunikaid Graphics
Project Managing Editor: Shari Howard McMinn (sharimcminn.com)

Publisher: AME, 1939 Plaza Drive, Suite 210, Parker, Colorado 80134
For more information on this and other titles from Generations and AME,
visit generations.org or ameprogram.com

Other books written by Mike Cheney:

One with Everything: Anatomy of a Hot Dog Stand and Other Great Family Businesses You Can Start
generations.org

One With Everything: Business Study Course
generations.org

TABLE OF CONTENTS

INTRODUCTION

By 1998, my wife had been homeschooling our children Annie (then aged 11-years-old) and Corey (then aged 7-years-old) for about 7 years. We had just relocated back to the metro area of Denver, Colorado from Scottsdale, Arizona where we had moved 10 years earlier for my previous job promotion. Long story short, we were back in Denver and had just opened a new multi-generational business: hot dog stands! That story is told in another book called, *One with Everything: Anatomy of a Hot Dog Stand and Other Great Businesses You Can Start*, which I wrote in 2017.

Our days consisted of my heading out to take care of the business while my wife took care of our home and taught the children their homeschool lessons. After about a year of this routine, my wife mentioned needing my assistance with teaching our children. She said she could use help with math and determining elective classes for them. We divided the kids' lessons between us, with me taking on math and Bible. She kept the remainder on her 'to teach' list which was, by far, the majority of the workload.

As the months rolled by, our children excelled at some subjects and struggled with others. I began to notice a pattern: they seemed to excel at those subjects which held their interest or were a part of everyday life but struggled with the rest. Clearly, some of this had to do with discipline, diligence, and just pressing on to master things whether or not they enjoyed them.

At the same time, there seemed to be a key to successful teaching which was being revealed in the process: instruct the student in a way that incorporates lessons into daily life. It seemed to be from this precept that relevance came, and from relevance our students were connecting to the teaching as being valuable to them now, and in the future. Hence, our children became more interested in learning. Cha-ching!

Great, we understood the principal. Now we had to make it relevant through application. From that point on, our homeschool journey changed for the better and the current success of my adult children in business, Christian faith, life, and relationships is the proof.

This study guide is meant to be used to teach, in real and relevant terms, the basics of earning, giving, saving, and spending money on a biblical foundation. Beginning with instruction on wisdom, character, and work — and their purposes and blessings — students will study and live the process of earning, giving, saving, and spending money. Thus, the first two chapters are topical studies of *The Book of Proverbs* and *The Book of Ecclesiastes*. This is because, *The fear of the Lord is the beginning of wisdom, and the knowledge of the Holy One is insight* (Proverbs 9:10 ESV).

This course can certainly be completed as an exercise without actually earning money or deploying it. However, my hope is that the students will use what they learn in this course to ACTUALLY deal with REAL money. If so, then the time you and the students invest in the teaching and learning counts as both formal curriculum study and practical application immediately and simultaneously. I believe this is the definition of applied learning.

Workbook Usage

Please see **Appendix B: Lesson Plan and Grading Template**. The work in the lessons has been divided and laid out in this template such that diligent and consistent work should result in the student completing the course in one 18-week semester. The suggested pace for this workbook is approximately 2.5 hours per week, totaling 45 hours, equivalent to one semester in a school year. Feel free to go at a quicker or slower pace as your family's schedule and student's ability permits.

The assigned tasks include "READING", "ASSIGNMENTS", "TESTS", "VOCABULARY" and "READ AND RECITE".

"ANSWER KEY/TEACHER NOTES" are labeled as such and contain both the lesson number and "READING", "ASSIGNMENTS", "TESTS", "VOCABULARY" and "READ AND RECITE" with answers and/or references in all cases.

This curriculum is in workbook format so the student can write answers to the questions on provided lines.
For additional work apart from this, I strongly recommend the student record and keep their work on virtual documents and spreadsheets for future reference. Hand-written work can be transferred to electronic files. Consider 'smart pens' and 'smart paper' to aid those who do better with handwriting their longer assignments. The act of writing helps retain knowledge further than mere reading. Their verbal explanation and/or discussions with peers and/or teacher will increase knowledge retention. Putting their knowledge into practice will cement what they have learned.

Relevant web addresses are printed throughout this workbook according to the subject matter being covered at that location. These represent references/citations to material used in the study guide and/or sources of more detailed information regarding the subject at hand. I have used sources which I believe to be reliable and have looked at the source web pages during the research for this study guide. I found them to be relevant to the subject and "safe." However, I can make no guarantee about that being the case in the future. Hence, parents/teachers are strongly encouraged to preview all web sources as they believe necessary to determine whether appropriate.

The students are encouraged to use this study guide and the herein referenced sources "open book style" when working on their "ASSIGNMENTS" and "VOCABULARY". The lone exception is the "VOCABULARY TEST" at the end of Lesson 6.

SCRIPTURE RECITATION

In each lesson, students are asked to read and memorize Scripture passages then offer explanations for particular verses. Please have your students recite each passage/verse at the end of their completed lesson then complete a written explanation. If they do not have it memorized, continue to have them work on it until they can recite it to you correctly. Remember, both recitation and writing are important tools to retain information learned.

ASSESSMENT AND GRADING

Because of the nature of the subject, the "fill in the blank" type answers are limited to vocabulary and terms. There are also some tasks where the teacher will simply check with the student to see whether the work is being completed. Most ASSIGNMENTS and Scripture recitations require some writing. These will constitute the majority of grading.

The majority of the student's work consists of creative/critical thinking with answers/explanations in brief essay form on worksheets which they will create and maintain. Accordingly, the answers will often be subjective. The teacher is looking for evidence of diligent work that follows a logical progression toward reasonable conclusions.

In the "ANSWER KEY/TEACHER NOTES" sections of this study guide, I have endeavored to provide examples of correctly structured answers based on the information from the text. The teacher should feel free to reveal parts of answers to the students when they need help understanding.

In all cases, the grading is percentage based (70%, 80%, 90%, etc.) with 100% as the perfect score. For example, if a vocabulary or budget spreadsheet test contains 10 questions and the student correctly answers nine, their grade would be 9/10 = 90%. Use your letter grade system equivalent if you choose.

For the assignments requiring essay or narrative answers, you will assign grades with percentages based on your assessment of the detail, reasoning, and conclusions the student reaches as follows:

100% (equivalent grade would be an A)

Content: Strong understanding of the assignment; directions followed well; detailed explanation with reasons; logical, strongly supported conclusions.
Format: Extremely neat and well ordered; quality and appearance is such that the document is suitable for a formal presentation.

90% (equivalent grade would be a B)

Content: Reasonably good understanding of the assignment; directions generally followed with some exceptions; somewhat detailed explanations and reasoning; mostly logical, somewhat supported conclusions.
Format: Not as neat as could be with a bit more effort/time; mostly well ordered; quality and appearance are such that document is acceptable for formal presentation.

80% (equivalent grade would be a C)

Content: Basic understanding of assignment; directions followed but with notable exceptions; explanations are a bit sparse and reflect some lack of effort; conclusions are mostly reasonable but limited by lack of quality research/explanation.

Format: Quite a lot of room for improvement; somewhat well ordered; might not be suitable for formal presentation depending on how picky the audience is.

70% (equivalent grade would be a D)

Content: Minimal understanding of assignment; directions followed in some cases; some explanations are reasonable but conclusions are definitely limited by lack of quality effort.

Format: The work that is complete is sloppy; the basics are there and someone reading it could probably figure out what the student is trying to say. Document is acceptable for oral presentation but not formal reading by others.

The grade can be further customized based upon the quality of the specific parts of content and format. For instance, the quality of specific parts of content of an assignment might be at the 80% level. However, the parts of the appearance/format (such as spreadsheets with all correct totals, appropriate columns, line item width, headings, and correctly utilized format for dollars, etc.) are at the 90% level. In that case the teacher might award an overall grade higher than 80% but less than 90%, ie; 83%, or a C+).

Work that grades out at below the 70% standard is unacceptable and should be reworked and resubmitted.

The final grade for the course is calculated on the weighted average of the various parts of study:

- Assignments and Tests - 50% (.50)
  Example: 5 assignments with scores 85 + 90 + 80 + 95 + 100 = 450; 450/5 = 90
- Vocabulary and Terms - 25% (.25)
  Example: 1 test with score of 90; 90/1 = 90
- Budget - 25% (.25)
  Example: 1 budget with score of 95; 95/1 = 95
- Final Grade = Assignments (.5 x 90) + Vocabulary (.25 x 90) + Budget (.25 x 95) = 91.25

If you prefer to use the non-weighted average to calculate the final grade, please feel free to do so:

- Final Grade = Assignments and Tests (90) + Vocabulary (90) + budget (95) = 275; 275/3 = 91.66

Convert the final percentage to a letter grade if you desire, e.g.: 91.25/91.66 = B+.

LESSON OVERVIEW

LESSON 1 – WISDOM AND CHARACTER

A brief study on wisdom and character using *The Book of Proverbs*. Students are tasked to read *The Book of Proverbs* and answer specific questions taken from the text.

LESSON 2 – PURPOSE AND WORK

Continues with Solomon's teachings as to work and God's purpose for it from *The Book of Ecclesiastes*. Solomon frequently used the phrase *chasing after the wind* when describing a man's efforts at accomplishing anything in life except that a man does so in the fear of God. Students will search the text to answer several questions and develop a proper understanding of work and its purpose.

LESSON 3 – MONEY: WHAT IS IT?

The definition of money, the concept and brief history of currency, and why it matters to one's daily life now and in the future.

LESSON 4 – EARNING MONEY

Beginning by answering the question "What does it mean to earn money?", the lesson continues with what the Bible says about the concepts of earning wages, provision and honor, and finishes up with some practical, flexible, and creative ways the student can earn money as opposed to working an hourly job for a company.

LESSON 5 – GIVING MONEY

Other than some vague ideas about kindness and generosity to others and "because the Bible says we should", there seems to be too little teaching to our children about the ownership and true stewardship of resources, including money. So, we ask and offer some answers to a couple of real basic, real relevant questions: "Whose money is it anyway?" and "Why do I need to give?".

LESSON 6 – SAVING AND SPENDING MONEY

It has been my experience that most people are not clear about the purposes and long term benefits of saving money. It's difficult to do something for the long term, especially things that are not pleasant in the short term, when you cannot see or relate to the benefits. It's even harder for young people to grasp because, well, they are young and often have little or no understanding of the passage of time and the influence that current decisions have on their future.

In this chapter, we split the concept of saving into small, easily digestible parts that allow the student to enjoy short-term success while giving him an appetite for the benefits of steady, consistent action over the long-term. Then we explain how saving is a part of spending and show the student how to create a spending plan (budget) for their earnings according to their goals and desires.

LESSON 1: Wisdom and Character

"The fear of the Lord is the beginning of knowledge;
fools despise wisdom and instruction."
Proverbs 1:7 (ESV)

INTRODUCTION

The Book of Proverbs teaches us about wisdom and character, the benefits of seeking after both, and the consequences of ignoring the teaching.

It's a difficult thing to account for wisdom in units of measure except to say that God did tell Solomon that he would be given wisdom exceeding any other king before or after his time.

READING

Read *The book of Proverbs.* (see **APPENDIX B**)

Assignment

Answer the following questions in narrative format. Include Scripture references with EACH answer.

1. Why was *The Book of Proverbs* written?

2. What are the components of wisdom?

3. What is the beginning of knowledge?

4. What are the benefits to those who seek and follow wisdom?

5. What are the consequences to those who do not seek and follow wisdom?

6. What does *The Book of Proverbs* say about wisdom and fathers/parents?

7. What does *The Book of Proverbs* say about diligence in work?

8. What does *The Book of Proverbs* say about the wise and the foolish?

9. What does *The Book of Proverbs* say about humility and arrogance?

10. What does *The Book of Proverbs* say about having a good reputation?

RECITE AND EXPLAIN

> **“If any of you lacks wisdom, let him ask God, who gives generously to all without reproach, and it will be given him.”**
>
> James 1:5 (ESV)

Answer Key/Teacher Notes

Lesson 1 – Wisdom and Character

Teacher Notes: The questions below show an example of what you are looking for in your student's work. The first few questions include a brief phrase answer with a Bible verse(s) reference. Although I have not shown this on all answers below, you should expect such from your student on his/her answers to all questions in this lesson and those going forward.

The answers should be written with enough detail to demonstrate a good understanding of the lessons from Solomon concerning wisdom and character. Since the text itself is the source of the answers to the questions, the student should include scripture references in their answers. The student is free to use Scripture references additional to those in the answer key.

Grading Suggestion: An answer without at least one Scripture reference is incorrect. Instruct the student to locate and insert Scripture references to missed questions.

READING

Read *The book of Proverbs*. (see **APPENDIX B**)

ASSIGNMENT

1. Why was *The Book of Proverbs* written?
   To know wisdom and instruction; Proverbs 1:2

2. What are the components of wisdom?
   Wise dealing, justice, righteousness, equity, knowledge, discretion; Proverbs 1:3-4

3. What is the beginning of knowledge?
   The fear of the Lord; Proverbs 1:7

4. What are the benefits to those who seek and follow wisdom?
   Find knowledge, discretion, righteousness; Proverbs 1:5-6, Proverbs 2

5. What are the consequences to those who do not seek and follow wisdom?
   Troubles of all kinds, life in foolishness; Proverbs 2, 3

6. What does *The Book of Proverbs* say about wisdom and fathers/parents?
   To be attentive to their teaching for they give wisdom, insight, and good precepts; Proverbs 4

7. What does *The Book of Proverbs* say about diligence in work?
   Proverbs 6:1-19

8. What does *The Book of Proverbs* say about the wise and the foolish?
   Proverbs 8, 9, 10

9. What does *The Book of Proverbs* say about humility and arrogance?
   Proverbs 11, 12, 16, 21, 22

10. What does *The Book of Proverbs* say about having a good reputation?
    Proverbs 22

RECITE AND EXPLAIN

James 1:5 (ESV)

Teacher, the concepts for the student to grasp are:

1. First we have to realize that we lack wisdom.

2. Then when we ask Him, God will generously give us His perfect wisdom.

LESSON 2: Purpose and Work

> **"The end of the matter; all has been heard. Fear God and keep His commandments, for this is the whole duty of man."**
> Ecclesiastes 12:13 (ESV)

INTRODUCTION

Measured as a tangible thing, monetary wealth is easier to tally than wisdom which is intangible. The Holy Bible describes Solomon's material wealth in several places. One current source estimates the modern equivalent of Solomon's wealth to be $2.2 trillion. 1 trillion is 1,000 billions. By comparison, the net worth of the wealthiest man in the world at the time of this writing (January 10, 2018), Jeff Bezos, Amazon CEO, was said to be worth $105 billion, approximately 1/20th that of King Solomon.

Retrieved from http://www.businessinsider.com/worlds-richest-billionaires-net-worth-2017-6

Retrieved from https://www.msn.com/en-in/money/photos/the-20-richest-people-of-all-time/ss-BBsg8nX#image=17

Despite his seemingly limitless material wealth, Solomon was despondent at the meaninglessness of life, *Vanity of vanities! All is vanity*, he declared in Ecclesiastes 1:2. Strong's Concordance says the meaning of the Hebrew word is "vapor". Other sources include these synonyms: delusion, emptiness, fleeting, mere breath, and useless. Several times, Solomon used the phrase, *chasing after the wind*, when describing a man's efforts at accomplishing anything in life except that he does so in the fear of God.

READING

Read *The Book of Ecclesiastes*. (see **APPENDIX B**)

Assignment

Answer the following questions. Include Scripture references with EACH answer.
What does *The Book of Ecclesiastes* say:

1. About pursuing anything, even wisdom and knowledge, for their own sake?

2. About the man, even the wise old king, who no longer accepts wise counsel?

3. Are the things God gives to man in order for man to live and be satisfied?

4. About the value of a good name (reputation)?

5. About the enjoyment of life?

6. What are the characteristics of the wise man and the fool?

7. What specific things did Solomon pursue in search of happiness?

8. What happens to material gains gathered for the sake of accumulating wealth?

9. What becomes of the person who pursues material gain or pleasures for their own sake?

10. Why did Solomon grow to hate his pleasures, his work, and his life?

11. What is the essence and conclusion to be learned from *The Book of Ecclesiastes*?

RECITE AND EXPLAIN

> "Whatever you do, work heartily, as for the Lord and not for men,"
> Colossians 3:23 (ESV)

Answer Key/Teacher Notes

Lesson 2 – Purpose and Work

Teacher Notes: The answers should be written with enough detail to demonstrate a good understanding of the lessons from Solomon. Since the text itself is the source of the answers to the questions, the student should include Scripture references in their answers.

Grading Suggestion: An answer without at least one Scripture reference is incorrect. Instruct the student to locate and insert Scripture references to missed questions.

READING

1. Read the book of *The Book of Ecclesiastes.* (see **APPENDIX B**)

ASSIGNMENT

1. About pursuing anything, even wisdom and knowledge, for their own sake?
   Chasing after the wind and folly; Ecclesiastes 1:16-18

2. About the man, even the wise old king, who no longer accepts wise counsel?
   Ecclesiastes 4:13

3. Are the things God gives to man in order for man to live and be satisfied?
   Ecclesiastes 2, 3

4. About the value of a good name (reputation)?
   Ecclesiastes 7

5. About the enjoyment of life?
   Ecclesiastes 5, 9

6. What are the characteristics of the wise man and the fool?
   Ecclesiastes 4, 7, 8, 9, 10

7. What specific things did Solomon pursue in search of happiness?
   Ecclesiastes 2

8. What happens to material gains gathered for the sake of accumulating wealth?
   Ecclesiastes 2

9. What becomes of the man who pursues material gain or pleasures for their own sake?
   Ecclesiastes 2:9-17

10. Why did Solomon grow to hate his pleasures, his work, and his life?
    Ecclesiastes 2:22-23

11. What is the essence and conclusion to be learned from *The Book of Ecclesiastes*?
    Ecclesiastes 12

RECITE AND EXPLAIN

Colossians 3:23 (ESV)

Teacher, the concepts for the student to grasp are:

1. We should work hard in whatever we do as a way to please and honor God.

2. We should realize He provides each work opportunity as a way for us to learn, grow, materially benefit and enjoy the people around us.

LESSON 3:
Money – What is it?

“For the love of money is a root of all kinds of evils. It is through this craving that some have wandered away from the faith and pierced themselves with many pangs.”

I Timothy 6:10 (ESV)

INTRODUCTION

I like the following definition of money from Investopedia:

“Money is often defined in terms of the three functions or services that it provides. Money serves as a medium of exchange, as a store of value, and as a unit of account. Medium of exchange. Money's most important function is as a medium of exchange to facilitate transactions.”

Retrieved from https://www.investopedia.com/insights/what-is-money/

Most of us refer to the bills and coins in our wallets and pockets as “money”. Although we know what we mean, that is not correct, strictly speaking. The bills and coins are actually just a convenient means to transfer some of our wealth to someone else in exchange for something else.

Let's say you head over to your neighborhood fancy coffee shop to order a fancy coffee drink. The person behind the counter says "Ok, that will be $5." You hand them a five dollar bill and they make and hand you the drink. Easy and convenient. (The same concept of convenience applies if you use a credit or debit card but with some VERY notable exceptions which I'll address later in LESSON 6 – Saving and Spending Money.)

Here's what really happened: You have a job which pays you $10 per hour. You work 20 hours in a week. You get paid every week. Your employer pays you for your labor in the form of a check made payable to you. The check is for $200. (I know we have not taken out the taxes, so the check to you would actually be less than $200. We'll skip the tax part to keep things simple for our example.)

A check is just money in another form. You take the check to the bank and exchange it for cash: $5, $10, and $20 bills. The bank teller gives you the cash because the check you got from your employer is written against his account at the bank which contains at least $200 worth of wealth. If you took the $200 check to the fancy coffee shop and handed it to them to pay for your fancy coffee drink, they would have told you to get lost. Here's why: you and your employer have agreed that you will accept his check in payment for your labor every week. However, the fancy coffee shop does not know your employer so they do not trust that his check will be honored by someone else when they try to use it to pay for supplies or other stuff they need to buy.

You see the problem: if everyone had their own form of money, it would be very difficult to buy and sell things because you would need to find buyers and sellers who would accept your particular form of money. Day-to-day living would be made much more difficult.

> "**For what does it profit a man to gain the whole world and forfeit his soul?**"
> Mark 8:36 (ESV)

You may have heard the saying "necessity is the mother of invention." That just means that when something needs doing, and the current means of doing it becomes more trouble than it's worth, then someone must figure out a way to get it done with less trouble, or else the need for the thing will just go away or, in the case of money, the entire economic system will not be able to grow and prosper. This is because of the economic principle of convenience. Read about it and how it relates to a lot of stuff in life in the book and study guide I wrote, *One with Everything: Anatomy of a Hot Dog Stand and Other Great Businesses You Can Start.*

Fortunately for all of us, some smart guys developed a form of money which is easy to carry around and recognized by nearly everyone as the preferred method to transact business. It is called the U.S. Dollar and is accepted by everyone in this country and most places around the world. There are practically no restrictions on its use, everyone recognizes it immediately, AND they have their own supply on-hand so you can get change back when you buy something. Pretty handy when you want a fancy coffee drink that costs $5 and you only have a $20 bill!

Most other countries have also developed their own forms of money. None of these other forms of money are as widely recognized or accepted as the U.S. Dollar, at least for now. All of these forms of money are called "currency." This is a convenient way of expressing that the money is used as a medium of exchange, a storage place of value/wealth, and an accounting system to keep track of who has how much and who owes how much to whom.

What would happen today if there were no forms of money or currency that everyone agreed upon as having a consistent value regardless of what was being purchased?

Let's go back to our fancy coffee drink example. You walk into your neighborhood fancy coffee shop because you've gotta have one of those fancy coffee drinks. How much does it cost? When we used U.S Dollars, the answer was $5. Now you and the coffee shop owner have to figure out another way. He might let you work for him for 30 minutes in exchange for the drink. Remember, we said earlier that you work for your employer for $10 per hour and that's also the going wage for new employees at the fancy coffee shop. Problem: you have to be somewhere else in a few minutes so don't have time to spend 30 minutes working to get your drink. You have your cell phone; no good because it's worth a lot more than $5. How about your belt? It's well used and you decide you can do without it, so you offer it to the coffee shop owner. He points to a rack of used belts in the corner and says he has not been able to resell even one of them. Discouraged, you leave the store. You get no fancy coffee drink and the shop owner gets no sale. Everyone loses. Sound far fetched? Well, that is exactly what took place before there were currencies. It was called bartering. It was clumsy and at the conclusion of the deal, someone usually ended up settling for something they didn't really want.

Because currency was invented, you are able to convert the value (cash the check) from the labor you provided to your employer into a medium of exchange that everyone accepts as payment (U.S. Dollars) and carry it around in your pocket. Pretty cool!

And that is the short answer to the question: "What is money?"

READING

1. Read this Investopedia article, *What is money?*

   Retrieved from https://www.investopedia.com/insights/what-is-money/

Assignment

Answer the following:

1. What are the three main functions of money?

2. Which of those three main functions is most important? Why?

3. What would be some of the negative results if there were no currency that everyone agreed to use?

4. What were some of the items people used to barter to transact business in the American colonies? What was the main reason these items were chosen?

Vocabulary and Terms

DEFINE: (See **APPENDIX A** for terms, definitions, and resource references)

1. Currency

2. Bartering

3. Money

RECITE AND EXPLAIN

> "Who can say, "I have made my heart pure; I am clean from my sin"?
> Unequal weights and unequal measures are both alike an abomination to the Lord. Even a child makes himself known by his acts, by whether his conduct is pure and upright."
>
> Proverbs 20:9-11 (ESV)

Answer Key/Teacher Notes

LESSON 3: MONEY – WHAT IS IT?

TEACHER NOTES: As the students' parent, you know them best. You are looking for the work to be completed according to the instructions. It is more important that the student grasps and demonstrates the ability to explain the concept than using the precise answer details and format given below.

READING

1. Read this Investopedia article, *What is money?*

   Retrieved from https://www.investopedia.com/insights/what-is-money/

ASSIGNMENT

1. What are the 3 main functions of money?
   Money serves as a medium of exchange, as a store of value, and as a unit of account.

   Retrieved from https://www.investopedia.com/insights/what-is-money/

2. Which of those 3 functions is most important?
   Money's most important function is as a medium of exchange to facilitate transactions.

   Retrieved from https://www.investopedia.com/insights/what-is-money/

   Why? Because of the convenience, speed, and ease with which transactions can be completed. If there were no agreed upon medium of exchange with agreed upon value we would have to resort to trading goods and services and experience all of the inefficiencies that would result.

3. What would be some of the negative results if there were no currency that everyone agreed to use? (Teacher, the example below is one possible answer. Your student might give a different example. The correct answer will adequately point out the pitfalls and problems and inefficiencies of doing business without a currency everyone agrees to use as a medium of exchange. Grade the answer based on the student's understanding and ability to communicate the problem.)

   Before the development of a medium of exchange – i.e., money – people would barter to obtain the goods and services they needed. Two individuals, each possessing some goods the other wanted, would enter into an agreement to trade.

   This early form of barter, however, does not provide the transferability and divisibility that makes trading efficient. For instance, if you have cows but need bananas, you must find someone who not only has bananas but also the desire for meat. What if you find someone who has the need for meat but no bananas and can only offer you bunnies? To get your meat, he or she must find someone who has bananas and wants bunnies ... and so on.

   The lack of transferability when bartering for goods is tiring, confusing, and inefficient. But that is not where the problems end: even if you find someone with whom to trade meat for bananas, you may not think a bunch of them is worth a whole cow. You would then have to devise a way to divide your cow (a messy business) and determine how many bananas you are willing to take for certain parts of your cow.

   Retrieved from https://www.investopedia.com/insights/what-is-money/

4. What were some of the items people used to barter to transact business in the American colonies? What was the main reason these items were chosen?

   (Teacher: The point of the exercise is that the student understands the concept that a medium of exchange needs to be useful to most people, easily transported and stored, and have a price that is relatively fixed/ steady and a referenced article is noted.)

   To solve these problems came commodity money: a type of good that functions as currency. In the 17th and early 18th centuries, for example, American colonists used beaver pelts and dried corn in transactions; possessing generally accepted values, these commodities were used to buy and sell other things. The kinds of commodities used for trade had certain characteristics. They were widely desired and therefore valuable, but they were also durable, portable, and easily stored.

   Retrieved from https://www.investopedia.com/insights/what-is-money/

   Other examples include: ammunition, flour, coffee, tea, salt, dried meat, and other staples that held up in long term storage and were widely used.

VOCABULARY AND TERMS

DEFINE: (See **APPENDIX A** for terms, definitions, and resource references)

1. Currency: a generally accepted form of money, including coins and paper notes, which is issued by a government and circulated within an economy. Used as a medium of exchange for goods and services, currency is the basis for trade.

   Retrieved from https://www.investopedia.com/terms/c/currency.asp

   a system of money in general use in a particular country.

   Retrieved from https://www.google.com/search?authuser=1&biw=1366&bih=657&ei= JcRXIGrEc7YsAWI0qP4CA&q=what+is+currency%3F&oq=what+is+currency%3F&gs_l=psy-ab.12..0i7 1l8.0.0..4546...0.0..0.0.0.......0......gws-wiz.Tuf7R1TY-C8

2. Bartering: in trade, barter is a system of exchange where participants in a transaction directly exchange goods or services for other goods or services without using a medium of exchange, such as money.

   Retrieved from https://en.wikipedia.org/wiki/Barter

3. Money: money is often defined in terms of the three functions or services that it provides. Money serves as a medium of exchange, as a store of value, and as a unit of account. Medium of exchange. Money's most important function is as a medium of exchange to facilitate transactions.

   Retrieved from https://www.investopedia.com/insights/what-is-money/

RECITE AND EXPLAIN

Proverbs 20:9-11 (ESV)

Teacher, the concepts for the student to grasp are:

1. No one can say their heart is pure or that they are clean from sin. If they do, they are lying or misled.

2. God hates and will not abide by or allow cheating to go uncorrected.

3. Every person reveals his character through what he does. Good conduct over a long period is a sign of good character. The opposite is also true.

LESSON 4: Earning Money

> **"Incline my heart to your testimonies, and not to selfish gain!"**
> Psalm 119:36 (ESV)

INTRODUCTION

What does it mean to earn money?

Here's what Webster's Dictionary says:

> **"Earn, to receive a return for effort and especially for work done or services rendered."**
> Retrieved from https://www.merriam-webster.com/dictionary/earn

In other words, when you do some work or provide a service to someone seeking to have the work done or service provided, you "earn" and are paid the agreed upon value of the work or service.

We learned in the previous chapter that you are normally paid in currency (U.S. Dollars) which you in turn can use to pay for work and services you desire.

There is a bigger, more important principle here than simply earning money. In *The Book of Ecclesiastes*, King Solomon said that earning money for its own sake is foolish, a chasing after the wind.

The bigger idea has to do with provision, specifically providing for those to whom you owe responsibility. Husbands are responsible to provide for their wives. Fathers are responsible to provide for their wives and children. Single people are responsible to provide for themselves. Everyone is responsible to provide for their widowed mothers and grandmothers in certain circumstances.

WHAT DOES THE BIBLE SAY ABOUT PROVISION?

The Apostle Paul wrote this to Timothy and the church at Ephesus:

> **"Do not rebuke an older man but encourage him as you would a father, younger men as brothers, older women as mothers, younger women as sisters, in all purity. Honor widows who are truly widows. But if a widow has children or grandchildren, let them first learn to show godliness to their own household and to make some return to their parents, for this is pleasing in the sight of God. She who is truly a widow, left all alone, has set her hope on God and continues in supplications and prayers night and day, but she who is self-indulgent is dead even while she lives. Command these things as well, so that they may be without reproach. But if anyone does not provide for his relatives, and especially for members of his household, he has denied the faith and is worse than an unbeliever."**
>
> 1 Timothy 5:1-8 (ESV)

At the base of it is the concept of honor. In verses 1-2, Paul admonishes the people not to rebuke the older man but to address him as if he is their father, to treat younger men as brothers, older and younger women as mothers and sisters and to do so in purity (honesty).

In verse 4, he makes it clear that the children and grandchildren of a woman whose husband has died are responsible for her provision, and that by "making some return to their parents" they show themselves as godly to their own households and please God as a result. In other words the children and grandchildren of the widow owe and are honor-bound to care for their widowed mother and grandmother.

After giving the principle and the benefit of joyful obedience, Paul warns the church that one who fails in this has denied his faith and is worse than an unbeliever!

Earning, provision, and honor are all tied together and involve much more than simply doing some work for someone in return for some money.

WHAT ARE SOME WAYS YOU CAN EARN MONEY?

The first thought that comes to mind for most people when they think of earning some money is to seek an hourly job for a company. Fast food places, restaurants, bookstores, and coffee shops are some of the more common choices. These jobs pay an hourly rate approximately equal to the federal minimum wage or about $10-$12 per hour as of this writing. So if you work 20 hours per week, you would earn $200-$240 per week. These jobs are plentiful in a strong economy, perhaps easy to land, and probably easy to keep if you show up on time, work hard, and take direction cheerfully.

Here's something you may not have realized: you can earn 50-100% more per hour by working for yourself providing services to people that they do not want to do for themselves! You don't even need to start a company. Just let people know you are available for work.

People in my neighborhood pay $15-$25 per hour to have other people mow their fields, clean out barns and stalls, take care of their animals, clean their houses, and do all sorts of other odd jobs.

I paid a young man $15 per hour to work two afternoons per week to trim grass, pull weeds, perform minor fence repairs, cut firewood, paint, and clean out our barn. He didn't even need his own tools because I was happy to let him borrow mine! This young man told me he was busy all week doing jobs like this for others in the neighborhood. I paid a lady $20 per hour to mow our fields. She said she is constantly booked out 2-3 weeks in advance with mowing jobs!

All they do to remain in demand is to post their availability or answer any number of the requests posted on Facebook ® and Nextdoor. Then, of course they show up to do the work and treat their customers well enough to receive callbacks.

> "**Wealth gained hastily will dwindle, but whoever gathers little by little will increase it.**"
> Proverbs 13:11 (ESV)

By comparison, companies charge their customers 2-3 times the wages they pay their employees. They have to do this to pay the expenses of running their businesses and make a profit on the work.

For example, if a company pays an employee $12 per hour to clean a customer's home they have to charge the customer at least $24-$36 per hour to provide the service. The housekeeping companies in my area must be busy with customers willing to pay those rates because there are many companies from which to choose.

There is an economic principle that says customers are always willing to pay less to get the same service they are receiving now. In other words, no one ever lost a customer by charging them less. If you are willing to clean houses, you'll have all the business you can handle by charging $20 per hour. Working 20 hours per week, you can earn $400 per week compared to $240 working the same number of hours at an hourly job. The concept and the math work exactly the same way no matter what service you decide to provide. You just need to be willing to hustle and work hard to provide excellent service.

READING

1. Read *How Young Entrepreneurs are Creating Their Own Wealth.*
   Retrieved from https://www.daveramsey.com/blog/young-entrepreneurs-create-their-own-wealth

2. Read *Need Extra Cash? 7 Fun Ways To Rake It In.*
   Retrieved from https://www.daveramsey.com/blog/need-extra-cash-7-ways-to-rake-it-in

3. Read *100+ Teen Money Making Ideas for Young Entrepreneurs*.
   Retrieved from http://juniorbiz.com/teen-money-making-ideas

Assignment

Answer the following, and ask for help with assignments 5 and 6:

1. What does the Holy Bible say about work in Colossians 3:22-24 and Exodus 20:8?
   Read the verses and write an explanation in your own words.

2. Explain why someone can make more money per hour working for themselves than working for someone else's business as an hourly worker.

3. List 10 services you can do for other people that will make you more per hour than you can make working at an hourly job.

4. Which 3 of those services best suit you? Why?

5. Start working and earning!

6. Open a checking account at a bank or credit union. Your parents' bank would be an excellent choice. Deposit your earnings into your account.

> **"Whoever is greedy for unjust gain troubles his own household, but he who hates bribes will live."**
> Proverbs 15:27 (ESV)

Vocabulary and Terms

DEFINE: (See **APPENDIX A** for terms, definitions, and resource references)

1. Customer

2. Earn

3. Entrepreneur

4. Provision

RECITE AND EXPLAIN

“ 4, But if a widow has children or grandchildren, let them first learn to show godliness to their own household and to make some return to their parents, for this is pleasing in the sight of God. 8, But if anyone does not provide for his relatives, and especially for members of his household, he has denied the faith and is worse than an unbeliever. ”

I Timothy 5:4, 8 (ESV)

Answer Key/Teacher Notes

LESSON 4 – EARNING MONEY

TEACHER NOTES: Primarily, two main concepts are being taught in this lesson: first, the link between earning and providing as shown in the text of I Timothy 5:1-8, and second, the concept of honoring with your work those in superior positions because of the command to do so expressed in Colossians 3:22-24.

Secondarily, you are working with the student to direct him toward practical earning opportunities which are in line with his passions, gifts, and abilities in order to give him the best chance to succeed.

READING

1. Read *How Young Entrepreneurs are Creating Their Own Wealth.*
   Retrieved from https://www.daveramsey.com/blog/young-entrepreneurs-create-their-own-wealth

2. Read *Need Extra Cash? 7 Fun Ways To Rake It In.*
   Retrieved from https://www.daveramsey.com/blog/need-extra-cash-7-ways-to-rake-it-in

3. Read *100+ Teen Money Making Ideas for Young Entrepreneurs*.
   Retrieved from http://juniorbiz.com/teen-money-making-ideas

ASSIGNMENT

1. What does the Holy Bible say about work in Colossians 3:22-24 and Exodus 20:8?
   (Teacher, the answers are in the text of the scriptures. Keywords/phrases include bond servant, work heartily, as unto the Lord, provide for his family, worse than an unbeliever, denied the faith. The student should quote the verses and write an explanation in their own words.)

2. Explain why someone can make more money per hour working for themselves than working for someone else's business as an hourly worker.
   a. Because companies charge their customers 2-3 times the wages they pay their employees in order to pay the expenses of running the business and make a profit on the work.
   b. There is an economic principle that says customers are always willing to pay less to get the same service they are receiving now. In other words, no one ever lost a customer by charging them less.
   c. By charging a rate less than companies charge but more than hourly employees make for doing the work.

3. List 10 services you can do for other people that will make you more per hour than you can make working at an hourly job.
   (Teacher, the answers can be from the reading assignments or the student's own choices.)

4. Which 3 of those services best suit you? Why?
   (Teacher, review these with the student to determine why he made the particular choices and whether you agree or would guide him in a different direction.)

5. Start working and earning!
   (Teacher, has the student started working towards this?)

6. Open a checking account at a bank or credit union. Your parents' bank would be an excellent choice. Deposit your earnings into your account. (Teacher, you may need to help your student arrange their schedule and provide transportation to accomplish this.)

VOCABULARY AND TERMS

DEFINE: (See **APPENDIX A** for terms, definitions, and resource references)

1. Customer: a party that receives or consumes products (goods or services) and has the ability to choose between different products and suppliers.
   Retrieved from http://www.businessdictionary.com/definition/customer.html

2. Earn: to receive as return for effort and especially for work done or services rendered.
   Retrieved from https://www.merriam-webster.com/dictionary/earn

3. Entrepreneur: one who organizes, manages, and assumes the risks of a business or enterprise.
   Retrieved from https://www.merriam-webster.com/dictionary/entrepreneur

4. Provision: the act or process of supplying or providing something: something that is done in advance to prepare for something else.
   Retrieved from https://www.merriam-webster.com/dictionary/provision

RECITE AND EXPLAIN

I Timothy 5:4, 8 (ESV)

Teacher, the concepts for the student to grasp are:

1. In verse 4, Paul makes it clear that the children and grandchildren of a widows are responsible for their provision. They are honor-bound to care for them.

2. In verse 8, Paul warns the church that one who fails in this provision, and specifically to his wife and children, has denied his faith and is worse than an unbeliever!

3. Earning, provision, and honor are all tied together and involve much more than simply doing some work for someone in return for some money.

LESSON 5:
Giving

> **“Each one must give as he has decided in his heart, not reluctantly or under compulsion, for God loves a cheerful giver.”**
> 2 Corinthians 9:7 (ESV)

INTRODUCTION

Take a look at this definition of giving:

> **“freely transfer the possession of (something) to (someone); hand over to.”**
> Retrieved from https://www.google.com/search?authuser=1&source=hp&ei=I7oRXOnZJ9LTjgT1-aGYDA&q=give+definition&oq=give+de&gs_l=psy-ab.1.1.0l10.3967.7068..8229...1.0..0.151.724.7j1......0....1..gws-wiz.....6..35i39j0i131j0i3.NwqxZFozzOU

I noticed the key words in the definition above, “freely” and “possession”. We know that freely means to do something voluntarily because you want to do so. Giving over possession just means that someone else gets to hold onto, use, and care for something on behalf of the owner. This is kind of a big deal because possession and ownership are not the same thing.

You lend someone a tool. They get to use it but do not "own it" because it does not belong to them. You did not give them ownership, only possession and use. You expect them to use it properly and not to ruin it or lose it.

If your neighbor came to your house asking that you give him your dad's car, hopefully you would say. "No." Why? Because the car does not belong to you. It is not yours to give.

What if your dad had told you that if the neighbor comes over to borrow the car, that you are to let him have the keys? Then you would be acting in obedience to your dad who told you to give the keys to the car to the neighbor. Why do you obey your dad? Because you know that he is the head of your family, he is wise, you love him, and you want to please him by obeying his wishes.

WHOSE MONEY IS IT ANYWAY?

The first verse in the first book of the Holy Bible states:

> "**In the beginning, God created the heavens and the earth.**"
> Genesis 1:1 (ESV)

It follows that, since He created the heavens and the earth, He owns them. The rest of Genesis 1 explains that God made everything that is in, on, and under the heavens and the earth, including you and me. Verses 26-31 tell us that God freely gave man the possession, use, and responsibility over the earth.

God knew that money would be something of great importance to people, something we would naturally want to hold onto. That might be one reason why money is mentioned more than 800 times in the Holy Bible. Here are a couple of verses:

> "**For the love of money is a root of all kinds of evil.**"
> I Timothy 6:10 (ESV)

> "**For where your treasure is, there your heart will be also.**"
> Matthew 6:21 (ESV)

WHY DO I NEED TO GIVE?

We will love those things which are most important to us, and if we LOVE money above God and other people, it will lead to a lot of other evils. Here are a few more verses:

> **Every tithe of the land, whether of the seed of the land or of the fruit of the trees, is the LORD's; it is holy to the LORD.**
>
> Leviticus 27:30 (ESV)

> **Bring the full tithe into the storehouse, that there may be food in my house. And thereby put me to the test, says the LORD of hosts, if I will not open the windows of heaven for you and pour down for you a blessing until there is no more need.**
>
> Malachi 3:10 (ESV)

> **We obligate ourselves to bring the firstfruits of our ground and the firstfruits of all fruit of every tree, year by year, to the house of the LORD; also to bring to the house of our God, to the priests who minister in the house of our God, the firstborn of our sons and of our cattle, as it is written in the Law, and the firstborn of our herds and of our flocks; and to bring the first of our dough, and our contributions, the fruit of every tree, the wine and the oil, to the priests, to the chambers of the house of our God; and to bring to the Levites the tithes from our ground, for it is the Levites who collect the tithes in all our towns where we labor.**
>
> Nehemiah 10:35-37 (ESV)

"Tithe" is the English word used to translate the Hebrew word meaning "one tenth". The verses referenced above use the word tithe and make clear that "tithing" was a command from God in the Old Testament. The references to cattle, grain, and produce (plants grown for food) were appropriate for the time the verses were written because the people lived in a culture and economy based on farming and raising animals. Income and wealth were based on these possessions. So people brought grain, animals, fruits and vegetables, wine, and oil to the temple (church).

The above verses also refer to bringing tithes to the church in season or "year by year". That makes sense because crops and herds were grown and harvested during certain times of the year. Today, most people earn money on a weekly or monthly basis and so their giving is done on that same schedule. If you get paid once per week, you would usually tithe once per week.

> **Honor the LORD with your wealth and with the firstfruits of all your produce;**
>
> Proverbs 3:9 (ESV)

The New Testament references to tithing are numerous as well: Matthew 6:1-4, Matthew 6:19-24, Matthew 23:23, and II Corinthians 9:6-10 are a few.

Many of the New Testament verses focus on the attitude we are to have about giving and not so much on the amount which is thoroughly addressed in the Old Testament.

I like what one commentator wrote in their conclusion about tithing/giving:

> **"God knows we are naturally inclined to be selfish and will want to keep our money. So while, yes, we should give cheerfully, sometimes we need to take the step and actually give regardless of our internal feelings. The act of giving allows God to change our hearts so that ultimately we end up doing so cheerfully. Many of us, if we let our natural minds decide how much to give, would likely opt for a lot less than 10%. Having a standard keeps us accountable."**

Retrieved from https://www.crosswalk.com/family/finances/is-tithing-for-the-new-testament-believer-11579309.html

So, we can say that the owner of everything (God) gives us the means to live (food, clothing, shelter) and the means to earn money to pay for them. He also tells us that we are to give back (tithe) a portion (1/10th) of what He gives us as He directs. He gives us 100% and asks only that we give back 10% of what He owns anyway.

READING

1. Read Matthew 6:1-4.
2. Read Matthew 6:19-24.
3. Read Matthew 23:23.
4. Read II Corinthians 9:6-10.

Assignment

Answer the following and begin work on completing assignment 6:

1. What does God say about giving cheerfully and for the right reasons?

2. What does God say about giving for the wrong reasons?

3. What does God say about trying to serve two different masters?

4. How much of your income should you set aside for giving?

5. To where does the Holy Bible say your giving should go?

6. Decide where your giving will be directed and start giving as you receive income.
If you have a checking account into which you deposit your earnings, you can write a check for the amount of your giving from that account. If you don't, you can just give cash from the amount you earn.

Vocabulary and Terms

DEFINE: (See **APPENDIX A** for terms, definitions, and resource references)

1. Checking Account

2. Debt

3. Giving

4. Saving

RECITE AND EXPLAIN

> **"Woe to you, scribes and Pharisees, hypocrites! For you tithe mint and dill and cumin, and have neglected the weightier matters of the law: justice and mercy and faithfulness. These you ought to have done, without neglecting the others."**
>
> Matthew 23:23 (ESV)

Answer Key/Teacher Notes

LESSON 5 – GIVING MONEY

TEACHER NOTES: The main goals of LESSON 5 are that the student understand the concepts of ownership (that God created and ultimately owns all things), giving (to hand over possession of something to someone else) and tithing (the percentage of income) freely, cheerfully (not out of a sense of legal or doctrinal obligation) and as God directs (primarily to the local church).

READING

1. Read Matthew 6:1-4.
2. Read Matthew 6:19-24.
3. Read Matthew 23:23.
4. Read II Corinthians 9:6-10.

ASSIGNMENT

1. Based on the reading, what does God say about giving cheerfully and for the right reasons?

   (II Corinthians 9:6-10) Each one must give as he has decided in his heart, not reluctantly. God loves a cheerful giver.

   (Matthew 6:2-4) Thus, when you give to the needy, sound no trumpet before you, as the hypocrites do in the synagogues and in the streets, that they may be praised by others. Truly, I say to you, they have received their reward. But when you give to the needy, do not let your left hand know what your right hand is doing, so that your giving may be in secret. And your Father who sees in secret will reward you.

2. What does God say about giving for the wrong reasons?

   (Matthew 23:23) Woe to you, scribes and Pharisees, hypocrites! For you tithe mint and dill and cumin, and have neglected the weightier matters of the law: justice and mercy and faithfulness. These you ought to have done, without neglecting the others.

   (Matthew 6:1) Beware of practicing your righteousness before other people in order to be seen by them, for then you will have no reward from your Father who is in heaven.

3. What does God say about trying to serve two different masters?

   (Matthew 6:24) No one can serve two masters, for either he will hate the one and love the other, or he will be devoted to the one and despise the other. You cannot serve God and money.

4. How much of your income should you set aside for giving?

   Definition of "tithe": 10%

5. To where does the Holy Bible say your giving should go?

   Primarily to your local church (Nehemiah 10:35-37, Malachi 3:10)

6. Decide where your giving will be directed and start giving as you receive income. If you have a checking account into which you deposit your earnings, you can write a check for the amount of your giving from that account. If you don't, you can just give cash from the amount you earn.

VOCABULARY AND TERMS

DEFINE: (See **APPENDIX A** for terms, definitions, and resource references)

1. Checking Account: a checking account is a bank account that allows easy access to your money. Also called a transactional account, it's the account that you will use to pay your bills and make most of your financial transactions. These transactions are debits to your account, while a credit is a deposit.
   Retrieved from https://www.thebalance.com/checking-accounts-2385969

2. Debt: debt is when something, usually money, is owed by one party, the borrower or debtor, to a second party, the lender or creditor.
   Retrieved from https://en.wikipedia.org/wiki/Debt

3. Giving: Freely transfer the possession of (something) to (someone); hand over to.
   Retrieved from https://www.google.com/search?authuser=1&source=hp&ei=I7oRXOnZJ9LTjgT1-aGYDA&q=give+definition&oq=give+de&gs_l=psy-ab.1.1.0l10.3967.7068..8229...1.0..0.151.724.7j1......0....1..gws-wiz.....6..35i39j0i131j0i3.NwqxZFozzOU

4. Saving: an amount of something that is not spent or used; savings: the amount of money that you have saved especially in a bank over a period of time.
   Retrieved from https://www.merriam-webster.com/dictionary/saving

RECITE AND EXPLAIN

Matthew 23:23 (ESV)

Teacher, the concepts for the student to grasp are:

1. We are not to tithe for the purpose of receiving praise and honor from other people.
2. To do so, causes us to neglect better things such as justice, mercy, and faithfulness.
3. We are to practice/live in justice, mercy, and faithfulness while tithing.

LESSON 6: Saving and Spending Money

> **"As for the rich in this present age, charge them not to be haughty, nor to set their hopes on the uncertainty of riches, but on God, who richly provides us with everything to enjoy."**
> I Timothy 6:17 (ESV)

INTRODUCTION

Here is what Merriam Webster says about saving:

> **"1) an amount of something that is not spent or used;**
> **2) the amount of money that you have saved, especially in a bank over a period of time."**
> Retrieved from https://www.merriam-webster.com/dictionary/saving

These are two correct definitions of "saving". Did you notice that they mean two different things? The first definition refers to what is leftover after you have finished spending. This definition says that spending comes BEFORE saving. The problem with following that definition is that you never actually get around to saving because in the real world there is not money left over once the spending is done.

A 2017 survey by the Federal Reserve (those are the guys who print and issue U.S. Dollars) found that 40% of American adults do not have even $400 cash available to pay for an emergency expense. In other words, they would have to borrow the money to pay for repairing their car, or a major appliance, or unexpected visit to the doctor.

Retrieved from https://money.cnn.com/2018/05/22/pf/emergency-expenses-household-finances/index.html

The second definition refers to money being saved (in a bank account) over a period of time. I like this definition because it strongly implies an intentional act performed repetitively and with good results. That person is referred to as a "saver". And it means they have developed the good habit of setting money aside for saving BEFORE spending.

I'M YOUNG – DO I REALLY NEED TO SAVE?

The best way to answer this question might be to ask a bunch of people older than you whether they wish they would have started and kept up the habit of saving money when they were your age. I think they would say, "Yes!" and that their lives would be better today, financially speaking, if they had.

Remember the survey that said 40% of them don't have $400 in cash? I don't think that means the other 60% are rolling in money. I know it's hard to imagine yourself being 20 or 30 years older than you are now. It was hard for me, too, but aging will happen. And you will be very glad to have started saving NOW!

> "**Precious treasure and oil are in a wise man's dwelling, but a foolish man devours it.**"
> Proverbs 21:20 (ESV)

WHAT ARE THE THINGS I SHOULD SAVE FOR?

Look, I know it's tough to imagine starting a habit if you think that it won't benefit you until many years in the future. It's even harder when that habit will cost you some enjoyment and freedom now. We'll cover time and compound interest and their positive effect on your money in another book in this series.

For now, let me just give you the good news: because you are young and have time on your side, you can save a "little money" steadily over a long time and that little money will grow up to be "big money" in 20-30 years.

More good news: because you are young and directing only part of your overall savings to your distant future, you will be able to save for more immediate goals at the same time such as a new laptop, phone, clothes, travel, a car, gifts for friends and family. You win now and later!

I'VE NEVER SAVED OR HAD A PLAN FOR MY MONEY – HOW DO I DO IT?

You save money by making a plan and getting started. A plan for money is called a budget. It means you figure out how much money you earn each week or month and then assign jobs to the money. Think of the dollars you earn as workers. You worked to get them. Now they are going to work for you. Give every one of them a job to do and then make sure they do it. Let's say you earn and are paid $200 per week ($800 per month). Then let's say you have some monthly expenses: cell phone bill, clothing, eating out, entertainment, gas, insurance and maintenance for your car, etc.

Write a list of your income and expenses (in order of importance to you but with Tithe and Saving at the top) by the week or month. I'll use a monthly list for this example:

BUDGET

ITEM	AMOUNT	IMPORTANCE
Income	$800	
Expenses		
Tithe/Give (10%)	80	1
Savings - distant future (10%)	80	2
Savings - near future (car, computer, etc)	150	3
Cell Phone Bill	40	4
Car Fuel	100	5
Car Insurance	100	6
Car Maintenance	50	7
Entertainment	100	8
Clothing/Grooming/Beauty	50	9
Emergencies	50	10
Total Expenses	**$800**	

> **"The plans of the diligent lead surely to abundance, but everyone who is hasty comes only to poverty."**
> Proverbs 21:5 (ESV)

Did you notice what happened?

1. Every dollar was assigned a job to do.
2. You planned for all of your known expenses.
3. You set aside some money for things that "just happen".
4. You put aside $80 for your future plus $150 for big purchases.
5. You lived on less than you earned.

Do this before the end of every month. In just 3 months you'll have $240 in long term savings, $450 saved for big purchases, plus $150 to take care of emergencies. Pretty cool! Those amounts will double in 6 months and after 1 year you'll have almost $3,000 in cash saved. All that happens after you gave/tithed almost $1,000 as the Lord instructs!

By giving each of your dollars a job, you decrease the chances of the money going somewhere you did not intend or know about. Most people don't know where their money goes each month. Because of this, they spend everything they earn and, usually, a few dollars more. When this goes on for a year they end up in debt. When it goes on for several years they end up in a LOT of debt. As of 2016, the average American household had more than $16,000 in credit card debt! They are paying more than $1200 per year just to cover the interest.

Retreived from http://time.com/money/4607838/household-credit-card-debt/

Earlier, I said we would review the way credit cards and debit cards work. A credit card is a rectangular piece of plastic which represents the terms on which a bank has agreed to let you borrow money. You order a fancy coffee drink and the person behind the counter makes your drink and charges you $5. You give her your credit card or swipe/insert it in a payment terminal. Technology allows the card to "tell" your bank that you want to borrow $5. The bank "tells" the coffee shop's payment terminal "OK" and makes an entry in the coffee shop's bank account and credits the account $5. You get the drink. The coffee shop gets the $5 from the bank. Oh, one more thing: you now owe the bank $5. Nice.

A few days or weeks later you get a letter (credit card statement) from the bank telling you they want their $5. They remind you that, according to the terms to which you previously agreed, you have a few days or a couple of weeks to pay the $5, along with the annual credit card fee of $25. They also remind you that, if you don't pay by that date, you will owe the $5 PLUS the $25 PLUS interest at the previously agreed upon rate. $30 for a fancy coffee drink. Not so nice.

> **"The rich rules over the poor, and the borrower is the slave of the lender."**
> Proverbs 22:7 (ESV)

No big deal. When you signed up for the card, the banker told you to pay by the due date and avoid the interest charge. Besides, the annual fee is a small price to pay for access to all the great benefits the bank offers to their "members." And don't forget how convenient it is to just whip out your card to pay for stuff. Much simpler than paying in cash. Plus you get to look cool in front of your friends.

That sounds like a nice theory. Problem: it rarely works out that way. Remember the $16,000 in credit card debt owed by the average American family? That same study says that those people would prefer NOT to owe the debt. But they do.

For most people, credit cards are just a trap for getting into debt. They would be much better off using cash they got from their checking account or a debit card linked to that same account.

The debit card works like a credit card except for one very important detail: it takes the $5 for the fancy coffee right from your checking account so you are NOT borrowing money from the bank. If you don't have the $5 in your account, you don't get the coffee.

The bottom line and main principle of this entire book is "stewardship." As stewards we are entrusted with the authority and responsibility for the property which belongs to our master, God.

READING

1. Read *15 Ways to Teach Your Kids About Money.*
   Retrieved from https://www.daveramsey.com/blog/how-to-teach-kids-about-money

2. Read *What is Biblical Stewardship?*
   Retrieved from https://www.ligonier.org/blog/what-biblical-stewardship/

3. Read *What is the Difference Between a Credit Card and a Debit Card?*
   From https://www.thebalance.com/difference-between-a-credit-card-and-a-debit-card-2385972

Assignment

Answer the following, then complete the project in assignment 3:

1. Why should I save some of the money I earn?

2. What is the main difference between a credit card and a debit card?

3. Create a weekly or monthly budget based on your income (earnings) and expenses.

Feel free to use the example budget in this chapter as your format. Your budget might have more or fewer items than the example. You can do this on a spreadsheet, with paper and pencil, or checkout Dave Ramsey's "EveryDollar" web based budget program (daveramsey.com). It's free and very easy. I have been using it every month since 2014. I like it because it is the easiest/simplest way I have found to manage my personal and business income and expenses.

a. Did you give every dollar a job? If you did then your budgeted income will equal your expenses.
If not then make adjustments so the totals match

b. Did you make giving/tithing your first expense? What percentage of your income is it?

c. At the end of each month, compare your actual income and expenses against your budget.
This is called reconciling and you need to repeat it every month.

Test - Vocabulary and Terms

(THIS IS NOT TO BE COMPLETED "OPEN BOOK STYLE")

DEFINE: (See **APPENDIX A** for terms, definitions, and resource references)

1. Bartering

2. Budget

3. Checking Account

4. Credit Card

5. Currency

6. Customer

7. Debit Card

8. Debt

9. Earn

10. Entrepreneur

11. Giving

12. Interest

13. Money

14. Provision

15. Saving

16. Stewardship

17. Wealth

RECITE AND EXPLAIN

> "Peter said, "Lord, are you telling this parable for us or for all?" And the Lord said, "Who then is the faithful and wise manager, whom his master will set over his household, to give them their portion of food at the proper time? Blessed is that servant whom his master will find so doing when he comes."
>
> Luke 12:41-43 (ESV)

Answer Key/Teacher Notes

LESSON 6 – SAVING AND SPENDING MONEY

TEACHER NOTES: The student's success with LESSON 6 will be measured by their diligence in saving and controlling spending through a budget. The written work in defining VOCABULARY TERMS and creating a well-ordered budget are important but secondary to the student actually earning, giving, saving, and spending according to a plan (budget).

READING

1. Read *15 Ways to Teach Your Kids About Money.*
   Retrieved from https://www.daveramsey.com/blog/how-to-teach-kids-about-money

2. Read *What is Biblical Stewardship?*
   Retrieved from https://www.ligonier.org/blog/what-biblical-stewardship/

3. Read *What is the Difference Between a Credit Card and a Debit Card?*
   From https://www.thebalance.com/difference-between-a-credit-card-and-a-debit-card-2385972

ASSIGNMENT

1. Why should I save some of the money I earn?

   So that I will: develop the habit of saving at an early age; accumulate money for my future and shorter term wants and needs; not spend all of the money I earn and then be always looking for more.

2. What is the main difference between a credit card and a debit card?

   You are borrowing money from the bank when you use a credit card. You will be required to pay along with interest and fees if you are late. With a debit card you are using your own money right from your checking account. You are not borrowing from the bank.

3. Create a weekly or monthly budget based on your income (earnings) and expenses. Feel free to use the example budget in this chapter as your format. Your budget might have more or fewer items than the example. You can do this on a spreadsheet, paper and pencil, or checkout Dave Ramsey's "EveryDollar" web based budget program (daveramsey.com). It's free and very easy. I have been using it every month since 2014. I like it because it is the easiest/simplest way I have found to manage my personal and business income and expenses.

a. Did you give every dollar a job? If you did then your budgeted income will equal your expenses. If not then make adjustments so the totals match

b. Did you make giving/tithing your first expense? What percentage of your income is it?

c. At the end of each month, compare your actual income and expenses against your budget. This is called reconciling and you need to repeat it every month.

(Teacher, check that the student has actually written out a budget similar to the one in the chapter. The format can be whatever the student/and you prefer: spreadsheet, paper and pencil, online program, etc. Check the math.)

VOCABULARY TEST (THIS IS NOT TO BE COMPLETED "OPEN BOOK STYLE")

DEFINE: (See **APPENDIX A** for terms, definitions, and resource references)

1. Bartering, 2. Budget, 3. Checking Account, 4. Credit Card, 5. Currency, 6. Customer, 7. Debit Card, 8. Debt, 9. Earn, 10. Entrepreneur, 11. Giving, 12. Interest, 13. Money, 14. Provision, 15. Saving, 16. Stewardship, 17.Wealth:

RECITE AND EXPLAIN

Luke 12:41-43 (ESV)

Teacher, the concepts for the student to grasp are:

1. Peter asks Jesus whether the parable about being ready for your master's return is for everyone or just the disciples. Well, clearly, this lesson is for everyone.

2. We should all conduct our affairs with excellence and on behalf of our master.

3. We should do this consistently so that we will be found managing the things to which we are entrusted even when our master looks in on us unexpectedly.

APPENDIX A

Bartering: In trade, barter is a system of exchange where participants in a transaction directly exchange goods or services for other goods or services without using a medium of exchange, such as money.

Retrieved from https://en.wikipedia.org/wiki/Barter

Budget: A budget is an estimation of revenue and expenses over a specified future period of time; it is compiled and re-evaluated on a periodic basis.

Retrieved from https://www.investopedia.com/terms/b/budget.asp

Checking Account: A checking account is a bank account that allows easy access to your money. Also called a transactional account, it's the account that you will use to pay your bills and make the most of your financial transactions. These transactions are debits to your account, while a deposit is a credit.

Retrieved from https://www.thebalance.com/checking-accounts-2385969

Credit Card: A credit card allows you to borrow money from a bank to make purchases, whether you're buying a burger or a round-trip ticket to France.

Retrieved from https://www.nerdwallet.com/blog/nerdscholar/credit-card/

Currency: Currency is a generally accepted form of money, including coins and paper notes, which is issued by a government and circulated within an economy. Used as a medium of exchange for goods and services, currency is the basis for trade.

Retrieved from https://www.investopedia.com/terms/c/currency.asp

A system of money in general use in a particular country.

Retrieved from https://www.google.com/search?authuser=1&biw=1366&bih=657&ei= JcRXIGrEc7YsAWI0qP4CA&q=what+is+currency%3F&oq=what+is+currency%3F&gs_l=psy-ab.12..0i7 1l8.0.0..4546...0.0..0.0.0.......0......gws-wiz.Tuf7R1TY-C8

Customer: A party that receives or consumes products (goods or services) and has the ability to choose between different products and suppliers.

Retrieved from http://www.businessdictionary.com/definition/customer.html

Debit Card: A debit card (also known as an ATM card, bank card, plastic card, or check card) is a payment card, made of plastic, which can be used instead of cash when making purchases. It is similar to a credit card, but unlike a credit card, the money comes directly from the user's bank account when performing a transaction.

Retrieved from https://en.wikipedia.org/wiki/Debit_card

Debt: Debt is when something, usually money, is owed by one party, the borrower or debtor, to a second party, the lender or creditor.

Retrieved from https://en.wikipedia.org/wiki/Debt

Earn: To receive as return for effort and especially for work done or services rendered.

Retrieved from https://www.merriam-webster.com/dictionary/earn

Entrepreneur: One who organizes, manages, and assumes the risks of a business or enterprise.

Retrieved from https://www.merriam-webster.com/dictionary/entrepreneur

Giving: Freely transfer the possession of (something) to (someone); hand over to.

Retrieved from https://www.google.com/search?authuser=1&source=hp&ei=I7oRXOnZJ9LTjgT1-aGYDA&q=give+definition&oq=give+de&gs_l=psy-ab.1.1.0l10.3967.7068..8229...1.0..0.151.724.7j1......0....1..gws-wiz.....6..35i39j0i131j0i3.NwqxZFozzOU

Interest: A fee paid for the use of another party's money. To the borrower, it is the cost of renting money, to the lender, the income from.

Retrieved from http://www.businessdictionary.com/definition/interest.html

Money: Money is often defined in terms of the three functions or services that it provides. First, money serves as a medium of exchange, second, as a store of value, and third, as a unit of account.

Medium of exchange: money's most important function is as a medium of exchange to facilitate transactions.

Retrieved from https://www.investopedia.com/insights/what-is-money/

Provision: The act or process of supplying or providing something; something that is done in advance to prepare for something else.

Retrieved from https://www.merriam-webster.com/dictionary/provision

Saving: An amount of something that is not spent or used.

Or, the amount of money that you have saved especially in a bank over a period of time.

Retrieved from https://www.merriam-webster.com/dictionary/saving

Stewardship: The office, duties, and obligations of a steward; the conducting, supervising, or managing of something; especially the careful and responsible management of something entrusted to one's care.

Retrieved from https://www.merriam-webster.com/dictionary/stewardship

Wealth: Wealth is usually a measure of net worth; that is, it is a measure of how much a person has in savings, investments, real estate, and cash, less any debts.

Retrieved from https://www.merriam-webster.com/dictionary/wealth

APPENDIX B

One Semester Plan – Two Quarters – Total of 18 weeks

Date	Day	Assignment	Due Date	✓	Grade
First Quarter					
Week 1	Day 1	**LESSON 1** – Wisdom and Character Read, memorize, recite James 1:5			
	Day 2	Read Proverbs Ch 1-4			
	Day 3	Read Proverbs Ch 5-8			
	Day 4	Read Proverbs Ch 9-12			
	Day 5	Read Proverbs Ch 13-16			
Week 2	Day 1	Read Proverbs Ch 17-20			
	Day 2	Read Proverbs Ch 21-24			
	Day 3	Read Proverbs Ch 25-28			
	Day 4	Read Proverbs Ch 29-31			
	Day 5	Lesson 1 – answer TEST questions 1-5			
Week 3	Day 1	Lesson 1 – answer TEST questions 6-10			
	Day 2	**LESSON 2** – Purpose and Work Read, memorize, recite Colossians 3:23			
	Day 3	Read Ecclesiastes Ch 1-3			
	Day 4	Read Ecclesiastes Ch 4-6			
	Day 5	Read Ecclesiastes Ch 7-9			

Week 4	Day 1	Read Ecclesiastes Ch 10-12
	Day 2	Lesson 2 – answer TEST questions 1-6
	Day 3	Lesson 2 – answer TEST questions 7-11
	Day 4	**LESSON 3** – Read INTRODUCTION
	Day 5	Lesson 3 – Read Investopedia article – "What is money?"
Week 5	Day 1	Lesson 3 – Re-read or continue reading Investopedia article – "What is money?"
	Day 2	Lesson 3 – complete ASSIGNMENTS 1 and 2
	Day 3	Lesson 3 – complete ASSIGNMENT 3
	Day 4	Lesson 3 – complete ASSIGNMENT 4
	Day 5	Lesson 3 – complete VOCABULARY
Week 6	Day 1	Lesson 3 – READ and MEMORIZE Proverbs 20:9-11
	Day 2	Lesson 3 – READ and MEMORIZE Proverbs 20:9-11
	Day 3	Lesson 3 – explain/write the meaning of Proverbs 20:9-11
	Day 4	Lesson 3 – explain/write the meaning of Proverbs 20:9-11
	Day 5	**LESSON 4** – read INTRODUCTION
Week 7	Day 1	Lesson 4 – continue reading INTRODUCTION
	Day 2	Lesson 4 – READING – Read "How Young Entrepreneurs are Creating Their Own Wealth"
	Day 3	Lesson 4 – Read "Need extra cash? 7 fun ways to rake it in."
	Day 4	Lesson 4 – Read "100+ teen money making ideas for young entrepreneurs"
	Day 5	Lesson 4 – ASSIGNMENT – complete assignment 1

Week 8	Day 1	Lesson 4 – ASSIGNMENT – complete assignment 2	
	Day 2	Lesson 4 – ASSIGNMENT – complete assignment 3	
	Day 3	Lesson 4 – ASSIGNMENT – complete assignment 4	
	Day 4	Lesson 4 – ASSIGNMENT – start assignment 5	
	Day 5	Lesson 4 – ASSIGNMENT – continue assignment 5	
Week 9	Day 1	Lesson 4 – ASSIGNMENT – continue assignment 5	
	Day 2	Lesson 4 – ASSIGNMENT – continue assignment 5	
	Day 3	Lesson 4 – ASSIGNMENT – continue assignment 5	
	Day 4	Lesson 4 – ASSIGNMENT – begin assignment 6	
	Day 5	Lesson 4 – ASSIGNMENT – continue assignment 6	
Second Quarter			
Week 1	Day 1	Lesson 4 – VOCABULARY – study vocabulary	
	Day 2	Lesson 4 – VOCABULARY – continue studying vocabulary	
	Day 3	Lesson 4 – READ AND EXPLAIN – begin I Timothy 5:4,8	
	Day 4	Lesson 4 – READ AND EXPLAIN – continue I Timothy 5:4,8	
	Day 5	Lesson 4 – READ AND EXPLAIN – continue I Timothy 5:4,8	
Week 2	Day 1	Lesson 4 – READ AND EXPLAIN – continue I Timothy 5:4,8	
	Day 2	Lesson 4 – READ AND EXPLAIN – complete I Timothy 5:4,8	
	Day 3	**LESSON 5** – INTRODUCTION – begin reading introduction	

	Day 4	Lesson 5 – INTRODUCTION – continue reading introduction		
	Day 5	Lesson 5 – INTRODUCTION – complete reading introduction		
Week 3	Day 1	Lesson 5 – READING – begin reading verses		
	Day 2	Lesson 5 – continue reading verses		
	Day 3	Lesson 5 – ASSIGNMENT – complete assignment 1		
	Day 4	Lesson 5 – ASSIGNMENT – complete assignment 2		
	Day 5	Lesson 5 – ASSIGNMENT – complete assignment 3		
Week 4	Day 1	Lesson 5 – ASSIGNMENT – complete assignment 4		
	Day 2	Lesson 5 – ASSIGNMENT – complete assignment 5		
	Day 3	Lesson 5 – ASSIGNMENT – complete assignment 6		
	Day 4	Lesson 5 – VOCABULARY – study vocabulary		
	Day 5	Lesson 5 – VOCABULARY – continue studying vocabulary		
Week 5	Day 1	Lesson 5 – VOCABULARY – continue studying vocabulary		
	Day 2	Lesson 5 – VOCABULARY – continue studying vocabulary		
	Day 3	Lesson 5 – RECITE and EXPLAIN – Matthew 23:23		
	Day 4	Lesson 5 – RECITE and EXPLAIN – Matthew 23:23		
	Day 5	Lesson 5 – RECITE and EXPLAIN – Matthew 23:23		
Week 6	Day 1	Lesson 5 – RECITE and EXPLAIN – Matthew 23:23		

	Day 2	**LESSON 6** – INTRODUCTION – begin reading introduction		
	Day 3	Lesson 6 – INTRODUCTION – continue reading introduction		
	Day 4	Lesson 6 – INTRODUCTION – continue reading introduction		
	Day 5	Lesson 6 – INTRODUCTION – continue reading introduction		
Week 7	Day 1	Lesson 6 – INTRODUCTION – complete reading introduction		
	Day 2	Lesson 6 – READING – read 15 Ways to Teach Your Kids About Money		
	Day 3	Lesson 6 – READING – read What is Biblical Stewardship?		
	Day 4	Lesson 6 – READING – read What is the Difference Between a Credit Card and a Debit Card?		
	Day 5	Lesson 6 – ASSIGNMENT – begin assignment 1		
Week 8	Day 1	Lesson 6 – ASSIGNMENT – continue assignment 1		
	Day 2	Lesson 6 – ASSIGNMENT – complete assignment 1		
	Day 3	Lesson 6 – ASSIGNMENT – begin assignment 2		
	Day 4	Lesson 6 – ASSIGNMENT – continue assignment 2		
	Day 5	Lesson 6 – ASSIGNMENT – complete assignment 2		
Week 9	Day 1	Lesson 6 – VOCABULARY – prep for test		
	Day 2	Lesson 6 – VOCABULARY – prep for test		
	Day 3	Lesson 6 – VOCABULARY – prep for test		
	Day 4	Lesson 6 – VOCABULARY – prep for test		
	Day 5	Lesson 6 – VOCABULARY – Test		
Final Grade				

www.ingramcontent.com/pod-product-compliance
Lightning Source LLC
Chambersburg PA
CBHW080609090426
42735CB00017B/3375
* 9 7 8 1 7 3 3 5 5 0 1 0 9 *